Y0-GUM-145
6748 9100 063 774 0
DATE DUE
5 16
DATE DUE
9 12 02
DATE DUE
.. 26 01

The SCOPES TRIAL

The SCOPES TRIAL

DEFENDING THE RIGHT TO TEACH

BY ARTHUR BLAKE

Spotlight on American History
The Millbrook Press • Brookfield, Connecticut

PHILLIPSBURG LIBRARY
WITHDRAWN
PHILLIPSBURG, N. J.
CHILDREN'S DEPARTMENT
Phillipsburg Free Public Library

Library of Congress Cataloging-in-Publication Data
Blake, Arthur.
The Scopes trial : defending the right to teach / by Arthur Blake.
p. cm.—(Spotlight on American history)
Includes bibliographical references and index.
Summary: In 1925 *The State of Tennessee* v. *John Thomas Scopes* became one of the most bitterly fought and important courtroom dramas ever played out in the United States. The trial raised such issues as freedom of speech, freedom of worship, the right to teach, and the right to learn. Darwin's theory of evolution and the argument for divine creation are discussed.
ISBN 1-56294-407-X (lib. bdg.)
1. Scopes, John Thomas—Trials, litigation, etc.—Juvenile literature. 2. Evolution—Study and teaching—Law and legislation—Tennessee—Juvenile literature. [1. Scopes, John Thomas—Trials, litigation, etc. 2. Evolution—Study and teaching—Law and legislation.]
I. Title. II. Series.
KF224.S3B53 1994 344.73′077—dc20
[347.30477] 93-37018 CIP AC

Cover photo courtesy of Brown Brothers.
Photos courtesy of UPI/Bettmann: pp. 12, 30, 31, 33, 38, 40, 44, 47, 49, 55; The Bettmann Archive: pp. 15, 21, 23, 24, 28; Brown Brothers: pp. 18, 36; AP/Wide World: p. 53.

Published by The Millbrook Press
2 Old New Milford Road, Brookfield, Connecticut 06804

Copyright © 1994 by Arthur Blake
All rights reserved
Printed in the United States of America
1 3 5 4 2

Contents

The SCOPES TRIAL

1

TRIAL CASE NO. 5232

On the morning of July 21, 1925, the jury filed back into the Rhea County Courthouse in Dayton, Tennessee. "Has the jury reached a verdict?" asked Judge John T. Raulston. "We have, Your Honor," replied the foreman. But as everyone knew, the verdict was a foregone conclusion. Neither the defendant, nor the lawyers, nor the nine hundred people in the courthouse, nor the thousands who had been breathlessly following the trial over the last ten days expected a surprise. No one had ever doubted the trial's outcome. Nevertheless, Trial Case No. 5232, *The State of Tennessee* v. *John Thomas Scopes*, was one of the most bitterly fought and important courtroom dramas ever to be played out in the United States.

The case that shook a nation had begun to take shape only a few months earlier. One day in March, Lucille Milner, the executive secretary of the American Civil Liberties Union (ACLU), was looking over the country's newspapers. An article caught her eye. It reported that Tennessee had forbidden the teaching of evolution in all public schools in the state. The theory of evolution, which had been set forth by Charles Darwin in his book *The Origin of*

Species, proposed that all forms of life change over time, and that man himself was descended from a more primitive organism.

The new Tennessee law, known as the Butler Act, stated that these ideas could not be taught in public schools, and that any teacher found guilty of teaching evolution could be fined between one hundred and five hundred dollars. That was a lot of money in 1925, when a Tennessee teacher earned only about eight hundred dollars a year.

The law was passed because some people in Tennessee believed that Darwin's theories contradicted the story of divine creation as recounted in the Bible. They brought pressure to bear on politicians who, not wishing to lose votes, agreed that evolution should not be taught in schools that depended on state funds.

But not everyone thought the state should have such powers. When Lucille Milner brought the news of the Butler Act to the attention of the ACLU's board of directors, they quickly decided that the law was unconstitutional. By making it illegal to teach evolution, the state of Tennessee was interfering with a teacher's right of free speech as guaranteed by the First Amendment to the Constitution. Also, they felt that the religious motives of the people behind the law challenged the idea of a separation between Church and State, which is also clearly spelled out in the First Amendment.

The ACLU had been founded in 1920 to protect the civil rights of minorities, the poor, and people who had trouble obtaining legal assistance. Having decided the Butler Act was unconstitutional, the ACLU placed a notice in Tennessee newspapers offering to pay the legal expenses of any teacher willing to test the law in court. Although this announcement caused tongues to wag all over the state, it was left to a half-dozen men in the town of Dayton, Tennessee, to do something about it.

Dayton was a small town like any other in the South, and the men who gathered in Robinson's Drug Store on the morning of May 5 were probably a lot like other men in similar communities. They included: George Rappelyea, a mining engineer; Fred "Doc" Robinson, the store's owner and chairman of the Rhea County School Board; Wallace Haggard, an attorney; and the Hicks brothers, lawyers named Herbert and Sue (Sue is not unusual as a man's name in the South).

The men discussed the new law and the ACLU's response to it. Why not test the law right here in Dayton, suggested George Rappelyea. Why not, the others chimed in. Sue Hicks was especially interested in arguing for the Butler law. But whom could they get to break the law and stand trial? The obvious candidate was William Ferguson, the principal of Central High School and its biology teacher. But Ferguson was a married man with children. He had too much to lose if he stood trial.

Then someone at the soda fountain mentioned John Scopes, the football coach and math teacher. John Thomas Scopes was only twenty-four, single, new in town, and well liked. At that very moment he was playing tennis with one of his students. A boy was sent to fetch him, and when Scopes arrived, still perspiring from the game, George Rappelyea came straight to the point: "John, we've been arguing, and I said that nobody could teach biology without teaching evolution."

The young teacher agreed.

Then Doc Robinson showed Scopes a copy of the *Chattanooga Daily News* that contained the offer from the ACLU. "Would you

In 1925, Dayton, Tennessee, was a quiet place. When people wanted lively conversation, they went to Robinson's Drug Store on Main Street to meet friends at the soda fountain.

be willing to stand for a test case?" asked Doc Robinson. "Would you be willing to let your name be used?"

Scopes hesitated, not because he was afraid but because he wasn't sure whether he had actually taught evolution. His duties were primarily teaching mathematics and physics. He had reviewed biology with the students only when he had substituted for Mr. Ferguson at the end of the term.

But the men in Robinson's Drug Store were willing to overlook this not so small point. They were mainly interested in having someone step forward and say that he had broken the law. Although the five men did not necessarily agree about evolution or about the constitutionality of the Butler Act, they all thought that a trial would bring new business and industry into Dayton. Such a trial could put the town on the map.

As it turned out, they got more than they bargained for.

2

AGAINST THE LAW IN TENNESSEE

When John Scopes returned to his tennis game that May afternoon, he was not particularly worried about having volunteered to stand trial. Even if he had broken the law, which he was not sure he had, he would still have gone along with George Rappelyea's plan. He believed he had a right to teach a scientific theory that just about every biology textbook in the country endorsed, including the one sold in Robinson's Drug Store. So even if John Scopes was not Dayton's first choice, he was the right choice.

John was born in Paducah, Kentucky, on August 3, 1900. When he was thirteen, his family moved to Danville, Illinois, and then moved again two years later to nearby Salem. In 1920 they returned to Paducah when his father retired. To understand John it is necessary to know something about his father. Thomas Scopes was a Londoner who came to America in 1885. He found a job as a railroad machinist and soon became an energetic fighter for workingmen's rights at a time when unions were very unpopular in the United States. Although a God-fearing man, Thomas Scopes was an independent thinker who subscribed to no organized religion. He had great respect for learning and every night read aloud

John Thomas Scopes was twenty-five years old when he agreed to stand trial in a case testing the constitutionality of the Butler Act—a Tennessee law forbidding the teaching of evolution in public schools.

to his young son from novels by Mark Twain and Charles Dickens. He also read from Charles Darwin's *The Origin of Species*, the book that introduced the world to the theory of evolution.

So John grew up with a lively and curious imagination. He graduated from the University of Kentucky with a Bachelor of Arts degree. He planned to become a teacher in his home state, but when a job opened up at the Rhea County Central High School in Dayton, Tennessee, he applied for it. For one hundred and fifty dollars a month, he would coach football and teach math and physics.

Dayton was a peaceful town situated in the Tennessee River valley. It had a hardware store, a furniture store, a small hotel, a movie theater, and "J. P. Darwin's [no relation to the naturalist] Everything to Wear Store." The main crops in the area were strawberries, corn, peaches, and tomatoes. The town itself was home to about 1,800 people, all of whom belonged to one or another Protestant church. There were perhaps two hundred African Americans in the vicinity, but no Catholics or Jews. Churchgoing accounted for much of Dayton's social life, and every Sunday a tall, skinny, blond man named John Scopes could be seen attending one of the services. Unlike most other worshipers, however, he was not a Fundamentalist.

Fundamentalism is the term applied to people who believe that every word in the Bible is true. Although it derives its name from a group of religious pamphlets—twelve small volumes called *The Fundamentals*—written from 1910 to 1915, Fundamentalism in America actually began earlier. In the 1870s many Protestants left their churches because their ministers did not automatically reject Darwin's theory of evolution. Instead, those ministers tried to adapt evolution to Christianity. But to many parishioners the Bible and evolution were incompatible. You could believe in one or the other but not both, and so any alliance with Darwinism was considered sinful.

According to the Book of Genesis the world was created about 6,000 years ago. God made man in His image in one day and all living creatures in two days. Since then, the Fundamentalists believed, nothing had changed; the various species of animals were said to be immutable. But Charles Darwin, an English naturalist, looked around him and observed that animals closely resembling one another lived on different continents, and that other animals, similar but not alike, lived close to one another. What, he wondered, could account for such variation in a species?

He concluded that all animals must have descended from a common ancestor that lived a very long time ago, and that since most species produce more offspring than can survive in one place—many succumb to disease, accident, predators, or lack of food—only those animals that adapt to the environment will survive and pass on their traits to the next generation. This theory is often referred to as "the survival of the fittest" or "natural selection." The fittest, however, are not necessarily the strongest or fiercest but those organisms best suited to live in a particular place and climate. A mosquito, for example, may survive where a lion could not.

Darwin outlined his theories in his book *On the Origin of Species by Means of Natural Selection, or the Preservation of Favoured Races in the Struggle for Life* (1859), more commonly called *The Origin of Species*. Because the book seemed to contradict the Bible's version of creation, Fundamentalists found its teachings immoral. They tried

This drawing shows God-fearing citizens, clergymen, and even animals fleeing in horror from Darwin, who is upsetting the universe with his immoral ideas.

to pass laws forbidding the teaching of evolution in public schools. Although such bills were defeated in a number of states, Tennessee finally passed one on March 21, 1925. The Butler Act was drawn up by state representative John Washington Butler, who argued that since public schools are supported by state taxes they should be responsible to the people who pay these taxes. And if the people think a certain theory is harmful, then they have a right to outlaw its teaching in school.

But legislation works both ways. If a law is passed on the local or state level and is thought by some people to fall outside the spirit of the United States Constitution, they can test the law in court. A state supreme court can overturn laws enacted by a state legislature. What the American Civil Liberties Union intended was to bring the case to a lower court, where they expected to be defeated. This then would allow them to appeal the case to the State Supreme Court of Tennessee. The ACLU's position was that the Founding Fathers had provided for a separation of Church and State in America, and it hoped that the State Supreme Court would overturn the Butler Act on this basis.

The First Ten Amendments to the United States Constitution are known as the Bill of Rights, and the First Amendment reads: "Congress shall make no law respecting an establishment of religion, or prohibiting the free exercise thereof; or abridging the freedom of speech, or of the press; or the right of the people peaceably to assemble, and to petition the government for a redress of grievances."

Therefore, the ACLU felt that the state of Tennessee could not dictate to the schools what to teach or not to teach on the basis of religious belief. No town or city anywhere had the right to pass an anti-evolution law, and the ACLU set out to prove that such a law was unconstitutional.

3

THE STAGE IS SET

When the men in Robinson's Drug Store urged John Scopes to stand trial for teaching evolution, they set in motion a train of events that almost overnight tranformed the sleepy town of Dayton into a hubbub of activity. Weeks before the trial was scheduled, people from all over the country began pouring into town. John Scopes remembered that they constituted "one of the rarest collections of screwballs I have seen in my life."

Peddlers arrived with cartloads of Bibles. Others came to sell small cotton monkeys and pins that said: "Your Old Man's A Monkey," since many people mistakenly thought that Darwin claimed that we descended from monkeys. Circus performers with chimpanzees showed up. Farmers and miners from neighboring towns came, as well as religious fanatics from all over who wanted to see the Forces of Good do battle with Godless Science. Dayton welcomed them with open arms. Main Street was decorated with flags and banners. Hot dog and lemonade stands were set up, and Robinson's Drug Store offered a new drink: "Monkey Fizz."

Of course, the media were there too. More than two hundred reporters converged on Dayton, as well as motion picture photogra-

The people of Dayton were delighted with the attention the trial brought to their town. Local vendors filled the streets with goods they sold directly from their automobiles.

phers from Hollywood. Twenty-two Western Union telegraph operators stationed themselves behind a grocery store and eventually tapped out two million words. For this was, despite the carnival-like atmosphere, an extremely important trial, whose outcome could affect the course of American education. In fact, only a trial of this magnitude could have procured the services of two of the country's most distinguished and charismatic individuals: Clarence Darrow and William Jennings Bryan.

In 1925, Darrow was sixty-eight years old and America's most famous trial lawyer. He had defended union leader Eugene V. Debs in the Pullman railway strike of 1894, which prompted John Scopes's father to join the machinists' union. And he was fresh from the celebrated Leopold-Loeb murder trial in Chicago in which he successfully pleaded for the lives of two young convicted killers. Darrow didn't think the defendants were innocent, but he believed that every person deserved a fair shake. He was one of the few lawyers of his day who defended African Americans accused of crimes. And when no one else would, he stood up for conscientious objectors (those who refuse to fight in wars because of religious principles) and for Communists.

Although Clarence Darrow talked in a folksy way and his clothes were always rumpled, he had a brilliant legal mind that he improved by constant reading. When a reporter asked Mrs. Darrow why she didn't buy her husband better suits, she replied: "I'll have you know that Mr. Darrow spends five times more on his clothes than you do. The only difference is, he sleeps in his." It was true—he often fell asleep while reading late into the night.

The Scopes case was made for a man of his abilities and convictions, and when he heard that William Jennings Bryan, the

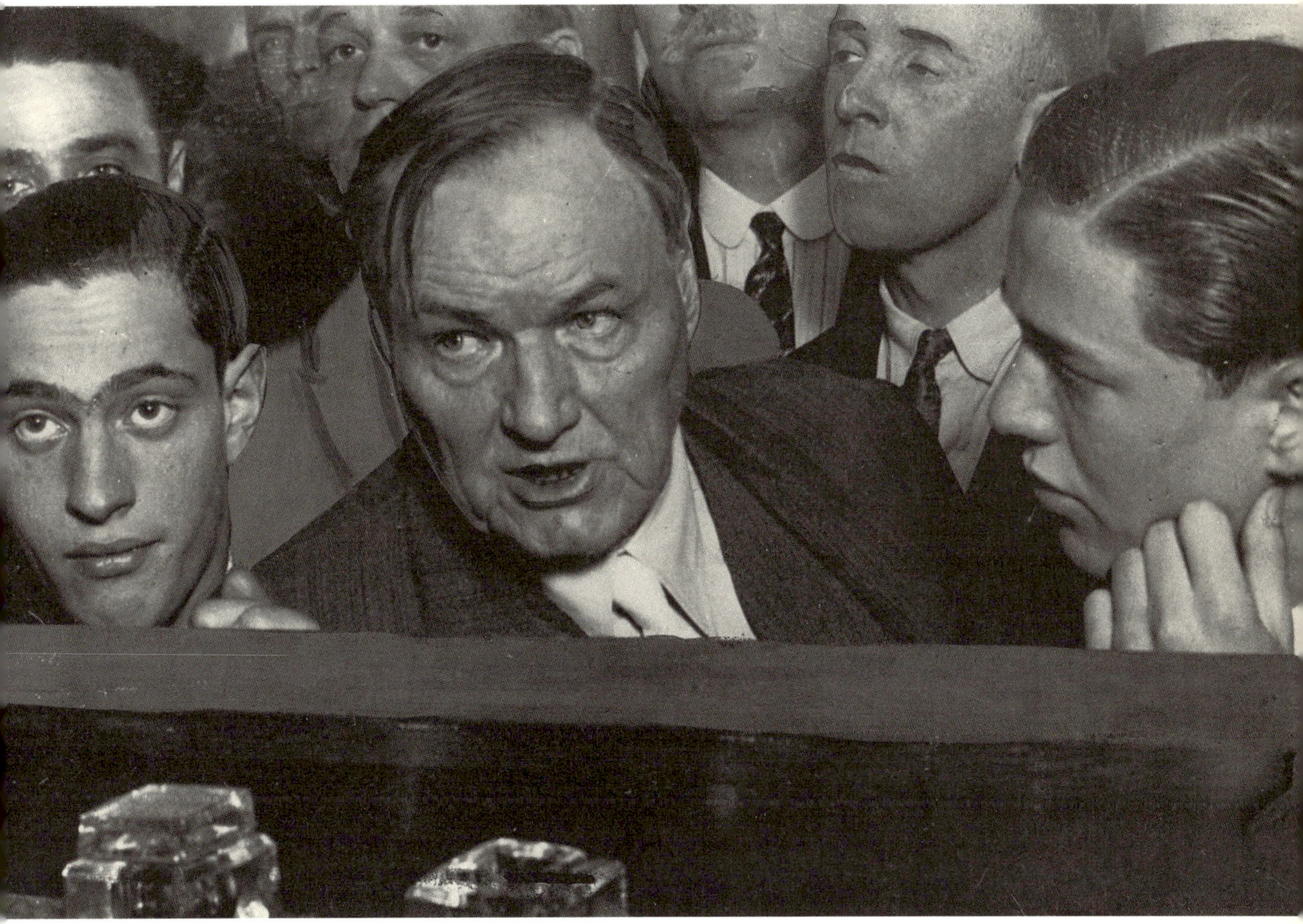

Clarence Darrow (center) was best known for defending Nathan Leopold (left) and Richard Loeb (right), two young men accused of the brutal murder of a fourteen-year-old boy in Chicago. Although found guilty, Leopold and Loeb were saved from the death sentence by Darrow's brilliant defense.

William Jennings Bryan, shown here at the 1896 Democratic Convention when he was running for president of the United States, was known for his speech-making abilities.

champion of Fundamentalism, had agreed to lead the prosecution, Darrow volunteered his services to Scopes's defense team.

Three years younger than Darrow, William Jennings Bryan was even more famous. As a state representative from Nebraska, Bryan had run for president three times—in 1896, 1900, and 1908—on the Democratic ticket. Although he never became president, Bryan served as secretary of state from 1913 to 1915 under President Woodrow Wilson and was both loved and hated for his liberal views. He favored a woman's right to vote (women were not given the vote in federal elections until 1920), a federal income tax, and the establishment of a Department of Labor. Because he supported farmers and workingmen against the interests of big business, he was known as "The Great Commoner." To his enemies, however, he was "The Great Windbag."

Like Darrow, Bryan was a wonderful orator whose voice could fill a stadium or soothe a crying infant. Unlike Darrow, he was deeply religious and took a dim view of evolution. Years before the Butler Act became law, Bryan had traveled around the country delivering a speech titled "The Menace of Darwinism," which summed up his philosophy:

> It is better to trust in the Rock of Ages than to know the ages of rocks; it is better for one to know that he is close to the Heavenly Father than to know how far the stars in the heavens are apart.

No two men were more alike in their respect for individual rights; no two men were more dissimilar in their attitude toward the Bible.

Although their names are not as familiar to us, other lawyers were also present at the trial. Representing the prosecution for the state of Tennessee were Wallace Haggard, Sue and Herbert Hicks, Benjamin G. McKenzie and his son J. Gordon McKenzie, and the attorney general for the 18th Judicial Court, A. Thomas Stewart. Also assisting was Bryan's son William Jennings, Jr.

The defense mustered an even more impressive team of lawyers, including Arthur Hays of the ACLU; John Neal, dean of the School of Law at the University of Tennessee, and his associate F. B. McElwee; and Dudley Field Malone, who had once served as an assistant secretary of state under William Jennings Bryan.

Although Bryan did not know it when he accepted the job of heading the prosecution, he had already run into John Scopes. Bryan had been born in Salem, Illinois, and often returned there to speak. In fact, it was Bryan who gave the commencement address at John Scopes's high school graduation. They would meet again on July 10, 1925, at the Rhea County Courthouse to take part in what became known as "The Great Monkey Trial."

4

"THE GREAT MONKEY TRIAL" BEGINS

The first day of the trial, a Friday, was reserved so that John Scopes could be formally accused of breaking a state law. The rest of the day was spent choosing a jury that would decide on his guilt or innocence. Presiding was Judge John T. Raulston, a short, chunky man who came each day to the courthouse carrying a Bible. Over the weekend, suspense came to a boil in town—and in towns all across the country.

On Monday, nine hundred people squeezed into a courtroom that was meant to seat only seven hundred. It was the middle of a Tennessee summer, and the crowded courtroom felt like the inside of a furnace. People fanned themselves with palm leaves and wiped the sweat off their faces with damp handkerchiefs. Soon all the men removed their coats, all except for the dignified Dudley Field Malone, who sat fully dressed in the one-hundred-degree heat.

The first order of business was the defense's attempt to "quash" (overturn) the indictment on the grounds that the Butler Act violated the state constitution of Tennessee. The defense

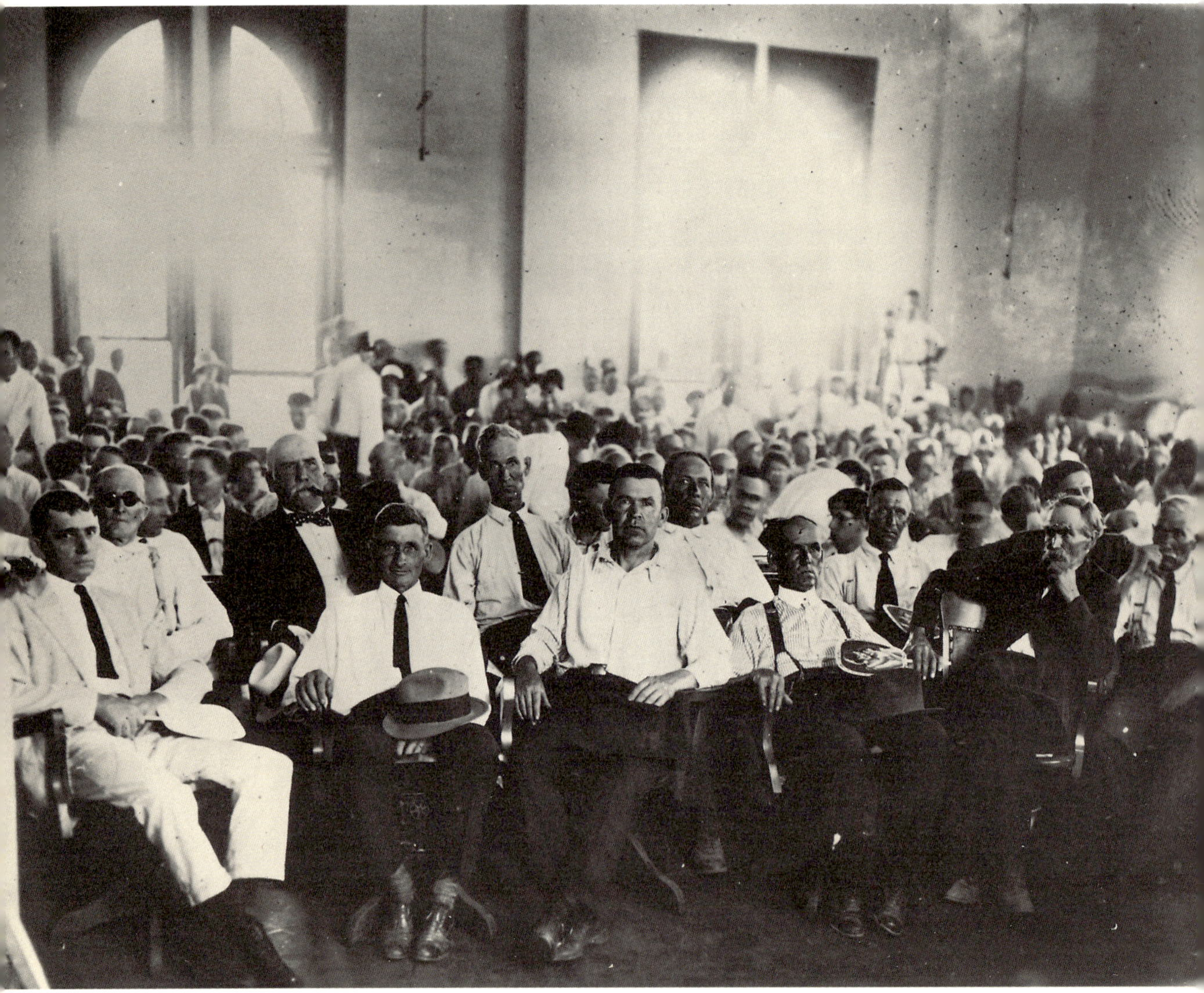

The courtroom was filled to overflowing with spectators who came to hear two famous lawyers go to battle over the right to teach.

claimed that any anti-evolution law restricted an individual's right to think freely, not only because it forbade the spreading of information but also because it infringed on the rights of those who believed in evolution or who wanted to learn more about it. Furthermore, the Butler Act was unfair because, while it prevented the teaching of evolution in the public schools, it said nothing about private schools. Shouldn't the law apply equally to all teachers in all schools?

The prosecution disagreed. It argued that the Butler Act was fair because the Bible was recognized throughout the land as a spiritual guide, and therefore no law that referred to the truth of Scripture could be wrong, so long as no one religion was given preference over another. The prosecution also mentioned other times that the state legislatures had told public schools what to do—and nobody had complained then.

But Darrow fired back. The Butler Act, he said, wanted to make the Bible "the yardstick to measure every man's intelligence, and to measure every man's learning." And this was not practical because the Bible could not confirm what man had learned about the universe in the past two thousand years. What did it know of astronomy, or chemistry, or mathematics? Darrow was not finished. Schools cannot be made to answer to any interest group, he argued. If they were, then Protestants opposed to Catholicism could forbid any mention of Catholic doctrine in the schools, and politicians could prevent views different from their own from being taught. In short, Darrow was cautioning the spectators: We have to be careful about what teachings we forbid because one day our own beliefs could be outlawed; one day the teaching of any idea could be a crime if enough people were opposed to it.

Bryan's lecturing tone and posture would become a familiar sight during the long days of the trial.

Over Clarence Darrow's objections, each session of the trial opened with a prayer. Bryan can be seen with his head bowed, standing behind and to the left of the microphone.

During this discussion the jury was absent from the courtroom. The judge had ordered it to another room because the motion to quash was strictly a legal matter on which he alone would decide. Monday afternoon ended with the lawyers still debating.

On Tuesday, Darrow started things off by objecting to the prayer that was read in the court each morning. Realizing that Darrow was trying to turn the case into a conflict between science and religion, Attorney General Stewart rose and said that as far as the prosecution was concerned this trial was not about science or religion; it was about the law. Did, in fact, a teacher in the state of Tennessee teach a doctrine prohibited by a state law?

Judge Raulston overruled Darrow's objection to the prayer, but the people's feelings were not soothed. They were angry at Darrow's anti-religion stance and threw him dirty looks. Darrow sensed their hostility. "They don't understand," he told a reporter. "I would fight for them as willingly as for anyone else. I would protect the right of a believer and unbeliever just the same."

The next day, Wednesday, Judge Raulston ruled against the motion to quash, saying he did not see how the Butler Act unlawfully deprived the defendant of "his liberties, privileges or property." He then turned to the defense table and asked, "What is your plea, gentlemen?" To which John Neal replied, "Not guilty, may it please Your Honor."

Attorney General Stewart's statement for the prosecution was brief. He maintained that Scopes had broken the law by teaching that man "is descended from a lower order of animals. Therefore, he had taught a theory which denies the story of divine creation of man as taught in the Bible."

Dudley Malone, still wearing his coat, spoke for the defense. He explained that the defense had both a narrow and a broad purpose. The narrow purpose was to prove Scopes innocent. The broad purpose was to demonstrate that the Bible was a theological tract and not a plan for education. "There is no more justification," said Malone, "for imposing the conflicting views of the Bible on courses of biology than there would be for imposing the views of biologists on courses of comparative religion. . . . Science and religion embrace two separate and distinct fields of learning."

Dudley Malone (second from right) in court. Judge Raulston is at the far left of the photograph, with Clarence Darrow and John Scopes to his left. Other members of the defense team stand behind Malone.

So even if Scopes had taught evolution, he was not defying the Bible, since science and religion were not in competition. "The defense maintains," Malone asserted, "that there is a clear distinction between God, the Church, the Bible, Christianity, and Mr. Bryan."

The jury was now let back into the courtroom and finally sworn in. The prosecution called to the stand Walter White, the superintendent of Rhea County Schools, who testified that John Scopes had acknowledged teaching the theories of Charles Darwin. Then two of Scopes's former students were asked to testify. They did not want to, thinking they could get their teacher in trouble, but Scopes assured them it was necessary for them to speak up. So they said that he had taught from the book that discussed evolution. And that was that. The state rested its case.

The trial, however, was far from over.

5

WHO NEEDS EXPERT WITNESSES?

After the state rested its case on Wednesday, the jury was once again ordered to leave the courtroom. The defense wished to call "expert witnesses" to support its side of the argument, and the judge felt that this testimony was not proper for the jury. These witnesses were prominent scientists and clergymen who had traveled to Dayton at their own expense to defend Scopes's right to teach evolution. But the prosecution opposed the introduction of their testimony.

In order for Judge Raulston to make a ruling, it was decided that one witness's testimony should serve as a sample. The witness called by Darrow was Dr. Maynard M. Metcalf, a respected zoologist who also happened to be a member in good standing of the Congregationalist Church. Dr. Metcalf explained the theory of evolution and noted that every scientist of his acquaintance believed in it.

But Stewart immediately protested that evolution, whether true or false, was not the point. The question was whether Scopes had broken the law. Although Judge Raulston probably agreed with Stewart, he allowed Dr. Metcalf's testimony to remain on the

The jury in the Scopes case, repeatedly sent out by the judge, spent more time outside the courtroom than inside.

record, at least for the time being. Arguments for including it and that of other experts would be heard the following day, on Thursday.

That day, prosecutor Herbert Hicks began by declaring that the defense was trying to turn the courtroom into a classroom, and since evolution was a theory, not a fact, expert witnesses were not necessary. He repeated the prosecution's position: The point of this trial was whether John Scopes had broken the law. Everything else was irrelevant. More legal hairsplitting now took place among the lawyers, and many spectators left the hot courtroom. Only the knowledge that William Jennings Bryan would address the court after lunch drew them back.

And that afternoon the courtroom was packed. All devout Christians in the area came to hear their champion speak. Although somewhat overweight and suffering from diabetes, Bryan still cut an impressive figure. When he stood up in his white shirt, black bow tie, and dark pants, the courtroom fell silent. With his fan in one hand and the school's biology text in the other, Bryan began by saying that he had not joined in the legal squabbling because in his opinion there was something far greater at stake here than the letter of the law.

He referred to the book, George William Hunter's *Civic Biology*, and drew attention to its charts and diagrams. He pointed to the circle on page 194 in which man was lumped together with 3,499 other mammals. Bryan didn't like this. How could a book read by children not distinguish between man and other animals? It was because of Darwin's misguided theories, Bryan said. "The Christian believes man came from above, but the evolutionist believes that he must have come from below, that is, from a lower order of animals."

Bryan then proceeded to make fun of *Civic Biology*. "How dare those scientists put man in a little ring like that with lions and tigers and everything that is bad?" As he spoke, it became apparent that he had no familiarity with the work of Darwin. All he cared about was that the Bible should not be questioned. He thundered that "parents have a right to say that no teacher paid by their money shall rob their children of faith in God and send them

Fan in hand, Bryan appears to listen respectfully to testimony during the trial. In truth, he tried to ridicule the defense.

back to their homes skeptical, infidels, or agnostics, or atheists." When he finished his speech, all the Fundamentalists cheered.

After a short recess, the court recognized Dudley Malone. Perhaps bored with all the legal wrangling, people in the courtroom were talking among themselves. The trial was not as exciting as they had hoped it would be. But then the dignified Malone did something that got their attention. He took off his coat, and with this simple and unexpected gesture he had the courtroom silent. He began mildly, pointing out that evolution did not mock the biblical version of creation or defy the basic principles of Christianity. But to demonstrate this conclusively, the defense had to call expert witnesses in order to explain fully what evolution was, and this the prosecution wanted to prevent.

Now he referred to his former boss, William Jennings Bryan, saying how much he admired Bryan. But then he went on to expose Bryan's ignorance of evolution. All that the defense wanted, Malone pleaded, was the truth—truth about evolution—and this truth must be heard because truth is greater than laws or government policies. "Why does the prosecution fear, so greatly, the teaching of science?" he asked. "For God's sake, let the children have their minds kept open."

When Malone finished, almost the entire courtroom burst into applause. It had been a stirring and powerful speech, and even Bryan knew it as he sat slumped in his chair. When Malone walked by him, he said, "Dudley, that was the greatest speech I have ever heard." Malone replied quietly, "Thank you, Mr. Bryan. I am sorry it was I who had to make it."

Whatever the merits of Malone's passionate speech, Judge Raulston ruled the following day, Friday, against allowing expert testimony, although he would permit such testimony to be read

Darrow was furious with Judge Raulston for seeming to side with the prosecution. Here he forcefully makes a point to an attentive courtroom.

privately into the record in case a higher court wished to review it. But he would not allow it to be heard by the jury in Dayton, because in his opinion neither scientific nor religious views were relevant. No one was surprised by this decision. Raulston, a Fundamentalist, had already shown where his sympathies lay. Yet Darrow could not contain himself. It seemed to him that the judge was overruling every objection made by the defense and sustaining every objection made by the prosecution.

Now it was Judge Raulston who became angry. "I hope you do not mean [that] to reflect upon the court," he said to Darrow, daring the lawyer to accuse him of being unfair. Darrow was not intimidated. "Well, Your Honor has the right to hope," he replied.

This bordered on contempt of court, and a furious Judge Raulston adjourned the trial until Monday.

6

THE BATTLE ON THE LAWN

Figuring the trial was all but over, many reporters left Dayton that weekend. Now that Darrow was not permitted to call experts to the stand, most people thought the defense would have to rest its case, just as the prosecution had done a few days earlier. The only suspense that remained was whether Darrow would be found in contempt.

The weekend gave time for the defense to read into the record the opinions of the clergymen and scientists they had hoped to question in front of the jury. It also gave time for Bryan to hold court outside the courthouse. He told anyone who would listen that there was a gigantic conspiracy against the Christian religion in America, but that he, William Jennings Bryan, would fight it until his last breath.

When the trial resumed on Monday, Judge Raulston formally charged Darrow with contempt and ordered him to post a five-thousand-dollar bond. He could, the judge said, defend himself the next day. After lunch, however, Darrow apologized to Raulston, and the two men shook hands.

The judge then made a surprise announcement. He ordered the trial moved outside to the courthouse lawn. He thought a crack had developed in the first-floor ceiling and was afraid that the ceiling might cave in. However, many of the people, unable to see the crack, simply thought that the judge wanted to get out of the sweltering courtroom.

Once the court was set up on the lawn, Darrow immediately objected to a nearby sign that said: "Read Your Bible." Tired of arguing with Darrow and wanting to move things along, Judge Raulston ordered the sign removed.

When things were ready to proceed, Malone turned to Scopes and whispered, "Hell is going to pop now." For at this point in the trial, Arthur Hays, the ACLU lawyer, stood up and announced, "The defense desires to call Mr. Bryan." At this, everyone on the lawn—reporters, farmers, wives and children, scientists, lawyers, priests and rabbis, the judge and the jury—froze in astonishment. This was unheard of, asking a member of the prosecution to testify for the defense.

Like a shot the prosecution lawyers jumped to their feet, objecting right and left—all except Bryan. When order was restored, he said he would be glad to take the stand, if he were allowed the same privilege with defense counsel. Bryan, of course, was in a trap. As the self-appointed champion of the Fundamentalists, he could not very well ignore Darrow's challenge. He had to take the stand.

Once again the jury was asked to leave because the judge felt Bryan's testimony might be inappropriate. The members of the jury, it has been estimated, actually spent only an hour in court during the entire trial. Excluded from hearing all arguments re-

On the seventh day of the trial, the entire court moved outside to the lawn. Clarence Darrow objected to the "Read Your Bible" sign visible on the courthouse wall, and it was removed.

garding matters of procedure, they missed Malone's splendid speech on Friday, and they missed the battle on the lawn.

Having taken his seat, Bryan nervously awaited Darrow's examination. But Darrow was not yet ready to pounce. He wanted to know how long Bryan had studied the Bible. Did he believe everything in it? Bryan said that he did. Did he believe that Jonah was swallowed by, and lived inside, a fish? Yes, said Bryan. Would he believe that Jonah swallowed a whale if the Bible said so? Yes, replied Bryan, although according to him the Bible made less extreme claims than the evolutionists.

Darrow now moved on to the biblical account of the Earth's creation.

DARROW: Does the statement: "The morning and the evening were the first day" mean anything to you?

BRYAN: I do not think it necessarily means a twenty-four-hour day.

DARROW: You do not?

BRYAN: No.

DARROW: You think those were not literal days?

BRYAN: I do not think they were twenty four-hour days.

DARROW: What do you think about it?

BRYAN: That is my opinion. I do not know that my opinion on that subject is better than those who think it does.

DARROW: You do not think that?

BRYAN: No. But I think it would be just as easy for the kind of God we believe in to make the Earth in six days as in six years, or in six million years, or in six hundred million years. I do not think it important whether we believe one or the other.

DARROW: Do you think those were literal days?
BRYAN: My impression is they were periods. . . .
DARROW: Have you any idea of the length of the periods?
BRYAN: No, I don't.
DARROW: Now, if you call those periods, they may have been a very long time?
BRYAN: They might have been.
DARROW: The Creation might have been going on for a very long time?
BRYAN: It might have continued for millions of years.

Bryan's last answer shocked and disappointed the Fundamentalists. To them a day was a day, twenty-four hours, no less, no more. To define a day as an indefinite "period" seemed to support the theory of evolution. What, they wondered, was Bryan thinking of?

Darrow had succeeded in showing that even Bryan did not believe without qualification every event in the Bible. He also managed, with further questions, to show that Bryan did not know enough about science to have any valid opinions about it. And when Bryan felt himself on uncertain ground, he became flustered.

BRYAN: I do not think about things that I don't think about.
DARROW: Well, do you think about things that you do think about?
BRYAN: *(confused)* Well, sometimes.

Finally, losing patience, Bryan charged that Darrow was trying "to slur the Bible." To which Darrow replied angrily: "I object to your statement. I am examining you on your fool ideas that no intelli-

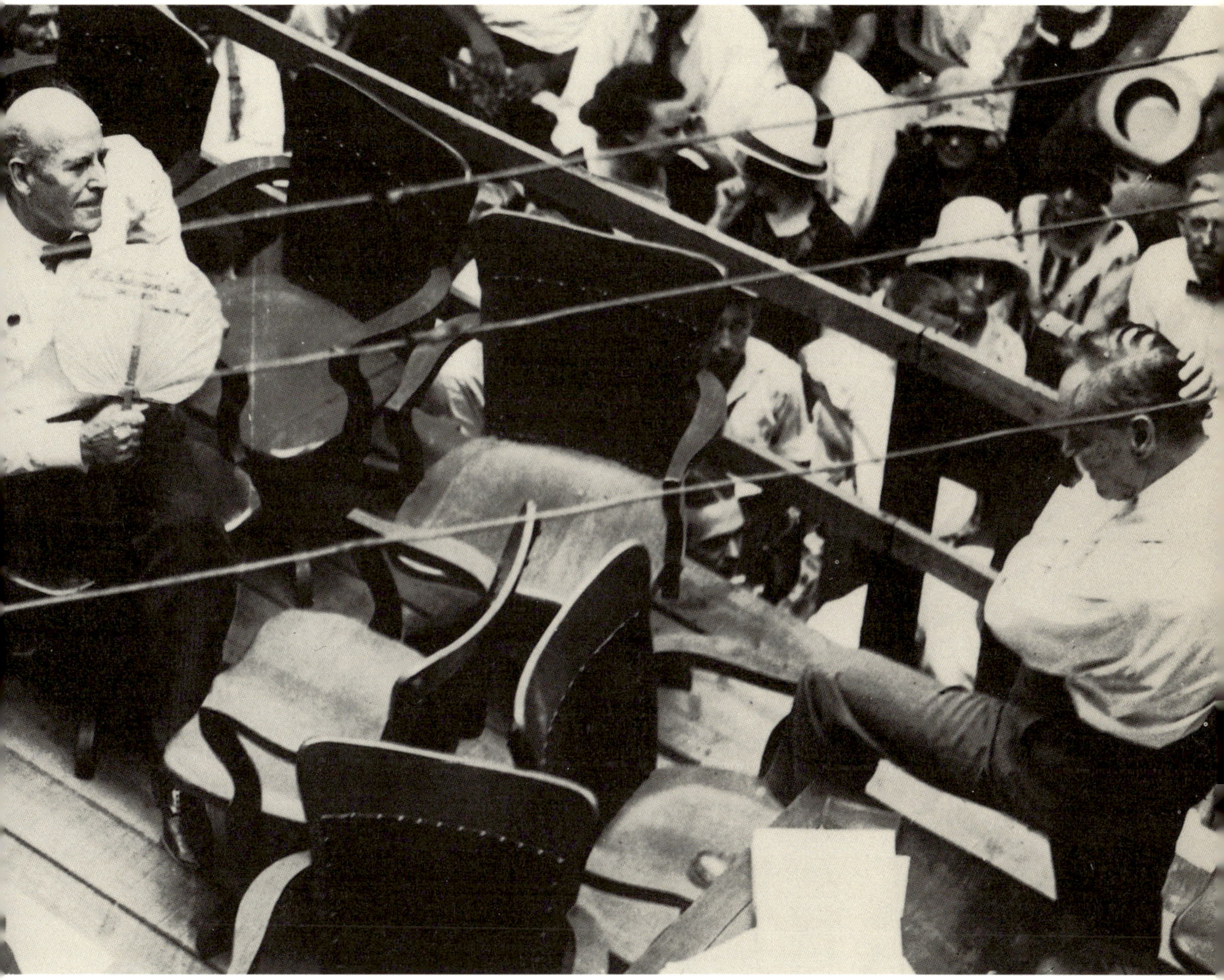

In one of the most famous scenes in trial history, Clarence Darrow (right) questioned William Jenning Bryan (left) about his understanding of how the Earth came to be created.

gent Christian on earth believes." At this, all the people on the lawn began grumbling and shouting while Darrow and Bryan stood in the hot sun glaring at one another. It looked as if a riot might break out, and Judge Raulston hastily adjourned for the day.

It had taken only an hour and a half. Two old men, representing two different ideas, met on a lawn in Tennessee to do battle. While one passionately and eloquently defended the truth of Scripture, the other coldly and logically repelled him at every turn. For the moment, it looked as though Clarence Darrow had beaten William Jennings Bryan.

The next morning Judge Raulston decided that Bryan's testimony was not relevant and ordered it removed from the record as if it had never happened. That meant that Darrow would not have to be questioned by Bryan. Raulston then asked that the jury be brought back. He advised the jury that it did not have to consider whether Scopes's lessons had conflicted with the Bible's version of creation, but only whether the defendant had taught that man is descended from a lower order of animals. If the jury found this to be the case, then it would have to find John Scopes guilty.

In other words, Judge Raulston was recommending that the jury bring back a guilty verdict, since Scopes had already admitted to teaching evolution. This was fine with the defense. It too desired a guilty verdict, because only a verdict of guilty would enable Scopes's lawyers to appeal the case to a higher court that had the power to repeal the Butler Act.

In fact, Darrow himself spoke to this point:

> The Court has told you very plainly that, if you think my client taught that man is descended from a lower order of animals, you will find him guilty. . . . This case and the

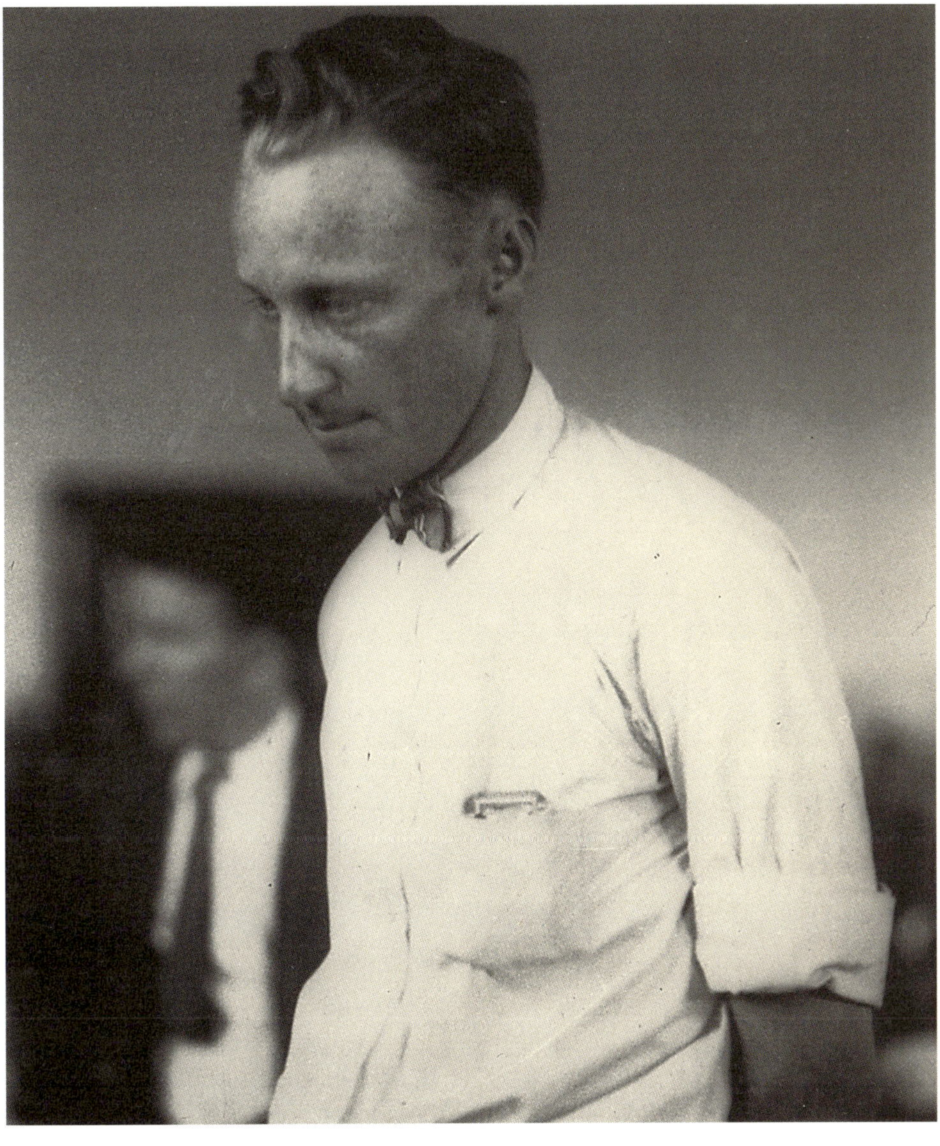

John Thomas Scopes listens as the verdict is read.

> law will never be decided until it gets to a higher court, and it cannot get to a higher court . . . unless you bring in a verdict. So I do not want any of you to think we are going to find fault as to your verdict.

Without coming out and saying so, Darrow had asked the jury to find his client guilty, and that's exactly what it did.

The judge now imposed a fine of one hundred dollars on John Scopes, who, having sat patiently for days, finally had his say in court. "I will continue in the future, as I have in the past," he said, "to oppose this law in any way I can. Any other action would be in violation of my ideals of academic freedom, that is, to teach the truth as guaranteed in our Constitution, of personal and religious freedom."

At 12:04 P.M., Tuesday, July 21, 1925, "The Great Monkey Trial" was over.

7

THE AFTERMATH

Dayton, Tennessee, returned to normal. The flags and banners were taken down, lemonade stands were dismantled, and the hotel once again had empty rooms.

Although Darrow had quickly left town, Bryan visited neighboring towns to give speeches. Returning to Dayton that Sunday, he ate supper and went to bed. That night he died in his sleep. Many people thought he had died of exhaustion or of a broken heart, but Bryan was a sixty-five-year-old diabetic who didn't take care of himself. Trial or no trial, he would probably have succumbed to diabetes fairly soon.

Now that Bryan was dead and Darrow involved in other cases, the spotlight fell again on John Scopes. Fan mail and hate mail flooded in. He received dozens of marriage proposals and one offer from a theatrical company to talk about evolution on the vaudeville stage. Although the fee was fifty thousand dollars, he turned it down. What he had fought for was too serious to trivialize.

John Scopes never taught high school biology again. A scholarship fund set up by a group of the expert witnesses enabled him to enter the University of Chicago, where he studied geology. Later, he married and took a job with an oil company and, fittingly, he spent the rest of his life studying rocks that silently bore witness to the Earth's real age. He wrote a few articles about the trial and also an autobiography that tells of his admiration for his father and for Clarence Darrow. He died in 1970.

In 1926 the ACLU brought *Scopes* v. *Tennessee* before the Tennessee State Supreme Court, appealing the lower court's ruling on Trial Case No. 5232. Although the State Supreme Court ruled not to overturn the lower court's decision, it did overturn Scopes's conviction on a technicality having to do with the amount of Scopes's fine. With the conviction overturned, the ACLU could not take the case to the United States Supreme Court. So the Butler Act stood.

Three other states now passed anti-evolution laws, but the rest of the states resisted or did not bother with such legislation. Nevertheless, the Fundamentalists got what they wanted. They had put fear into the hearts of educators and publishers, who had to think twice before teaching or printing Darwin's theories.

In fact, it was not until the 1960s that biology texts again began seriously addressing the question of evolution. The reason was that America felt it was falling behind the Soviet Union on matters of education. Russia, after all, had just launched the first manned satellite into space. Science was too important to neglect, and in 1967 the Butler Act was finally repealed by the Tennessee state legislature, and shortly thereafter anti-evolution laws in other states met the same fate.

In the 1960s, schools in some states were beginning to allow students access to texts such as these on biology and Darwinism. But, as recently as 1980, many southern states, including Louisiana and Arkansas, were still struggling with the concept of evolution being taught in public schools.

But the Fundamentalists were not finished. Realizing they could not dismiss science as easily as they had in 1925, they offered a counter theory to evolution, which they called Scientific Creationism. They argued that this too was a scientific theory, one that supported the biblical version of creation. Shrewdly, they did not demand that the schools stop teaching evolution; they demanded only that Scientific Creationism be taught alongside Darwin's theories, and in the early 1980s laws requiring the teaching of this new "theory" were passed in Louisiana and Arkansas.

Once again the ACLU stepped in. It challenged the Arkansas law on the grounds that Scientific Creationism was not really a science but a religious doctrine. Therefore, any law requiring its inclusion in a school curriculum was unconstitutional because it violated the separation between Church and State. This time, expert witnesses on both sides were allowed to testify, and it quickly became clear which of the two theories was backed up by solid evidence. The law was overturned.

During these hearings the name of John Scopes was, if not always said aloud, remembered. "The Great Monkey Trial" had not been forgotten. A play had been written about it that ran on Broadway in 1955, and a movie, *Inherit the Wind*, based on the play, opened in Dayton, Tennessee, in 1960. Attending the premiere was John Thomas Scopes.

By the time of the movie's premiere, many of the trial's principal actors were no longer alive. Gone were Darrow, Malone, Hays, Neal, and Judge Raulston. George Rappelyea, whose idea it had all been thirty-five years before, had moved away. Doc Robinson was dead too, but his drugstore was still there, and it had a new drink: a "Scopes Soda" for fifteen cents. Many things were

In 1960, John Thomas Scopes returned to Dayton, Tennessee, to attend the premiere of the movie based on his trial. Here he and his wife and a friend enjoy sodas at Robinson's Drug Store on Scopes Trial Day, July 21, 1960.

different, but some were not. Teachers in Rhea County in 1960 were still required to sign a pledge that they would not teach evolution. One has to wonder about John Scopes's reaction when the mayor of Dayton proclaimed a Scopes Trial Day on July 21, 1960, and presented him with the key to the city.

8

WHO WAS RIGHT?

In 1991 a cross section of Americans were asked in a Gallup poll about their religious beliefs and their feelings about evolution. Forty-seven percent said they believed in the biblical version of creation, while forty percent said they believed that man developed from less advanced organisms over millions of years, although God had a hand in this process.

There are still many people, perhaps even half the country, who dispute the theory of evolution. Taking the Bible literally, they believe that God created the Earth and man and all the animals about six thousand years ago, despite the physical evidence supplied by rocks and fossils that indicates that the Earth is hundreds of millions of years old.

Their reasons are not based on scientific fact. They believe, as Bryan had believed seventy years before, that the Bible is the word of God and therefore must be true. Today, many remember Bryan as a narrow and ignorant man. But was he wrong to argue the way he did? Were his ideas, as Darrow said, merely "fool ideas that no intelligent Christian on earth believes"? For this would mean that almost fifty percent of Americans are unintelligent.

AN ONGOING

The debate between people who believe in divine creation and those who accept the theory of evolution continues to rage. Points can be made for both sides.

The argument for the divine creation of human beings has a strong emotional appeal to many people.

Because *Homo sapiens* are the only creatures on Earth who are capable of knowing God, why would God have waited millions of years for them to evolve? And if *Homo sapiens* are the only creatures capable of worshiping God, would their ancestors have been microbes or monkeys?

In the Book of Genesis it says that God created man in His image. To question this is to question every statement in the Bible. People who believe the Bible to be true, believe it must be true in every respect. It is the word of God, and to doubt one word of it is to doubt the existence of God Himself. And if God exists, then the Bible, including the story of the divine creation, is true.

ARGUMENT

The theory of evolution itself is generally accepted among scientists, although there is not always agreement on why a certain species evolves or becomes extinct. The evidence for evolution can be summed up as follows:

Geologists have been able to determine the approximate age of the Earth by measuring the amounts of certain radioactive elements in rocks.

Rocks themselves form and erode over time. The oldest rock formations lie beneath later ones.

Embedded in these layers of rock are fossils, or the skeletonized remains of plants and animals. The older the rock layer, the older the animals whose fossils are found there.

Fossils themselves reveal the physical development of a species. Although the fossil records may be incomplete, scientists have been able to trace the development of life forms from early times to the present. From examining the fossils of horses, for example, scientists can get a picture of the many stages of the horse's evolution, beginning with its earliest ancestor, *Eohippus*, which lived 55 million years ago.

It is perhaps impossible to answer such a question to everyone's satisfaction. We believe what we choose to believe because of what is important to us. People who accept the word of the Bible and who accept the existence of miracles do not rely on reason or evidence. Faith is, after all, what makes all things possible. For example, if one believes in an omnipotent God, a God who can do anything, then such a God could have created the Earth six thousand years ago and then aged it to make it seem much older.

Whether the Bible is true in all or some respects, or whether evolution is true, finally has little to do with the way we run our schools. The real issue is whether any one person or group has a right to say what should or should not be taught. This is a nation whose Constitution says that the State and the Church should remain separate, that neither should interfere with the rights of the other.

We are "One Nation Under God," states the Pledge of Allegiance. But this does not mean that everyone must read the Bible or interpret it in the same way. Nor does it mean that we must agree with everything that our teachers tell us, if it conflicts with our religious beliefs. We are free to believe what we want to believe, yet we must also allow teachers the opportunity to acquaint us with the knowledge discovered by scholars, researchers, and scientists in every discipline.

"You can only be free if I am free," declared Clarence Darrow. If even one person's freedom is limited, if just one person is deprived of his or her right to speak or to learn, then the liberty of *all* people is threatened. It is this basic freedom that John Scopes fought to win in 1925, and it is this freedom that we must fight to preserve today.

Chronology

1859	Charles Darwin's book *The Origin of Species* is published.
August 3, 1900	John Thomas Scopes is born in Paducah, Kentucky.
1910 to 1915	The twelve religious pamphlets called *The Fundamentals* are published.
March 21, 1925	The Butler Act is passed, forbidding the teaching of evolution in public schools in Tennessee.
July 10, 1925	Trial Case No. 5232, *The State of Tennessee* v. *John Thomas Scopes*, begins.
July 21, 1925	Scopes is found guilty of teaching evolution.
1926	Scopes's conviction is overturned on appeal to the Tennessee State Supreme Court.
1960	The movie *Inherit the Wind*, based on "The Great Monkey Trial," opens.
July 21, 1960	Scopes Trial Day is declared in Dayton, Tennessee.
1967	The Butler Act is repealed by the Tennessee state legislature.
October 21, 1970	John Thomas Scopes dies.

Bibliography

*Books for children.

*Bailey, Marilyn. *Evolution: Opposing Viewpoints.* San Diego: Greenhaven Press, 1990.

*Childers, Norman H. *The Great Monkey Debate.* Memphis: White Rose Press, 1988.

De Camp, Sprague L. *The Great Monkey Trial.* New York: Doubleday, 1968.

Dickler, Gerald. *Man on Trial.* New York: Doubleday, 1962.

Ginger, Ray. *Six Days or Forever.* New York: Oxford University Press, 1974.

Kaplan, Morris. *Six Trials.* New York: Thomas Y. Crowell, 1969.

*McGowan, Tom. *The Great Monkey Trial.* New York: Franklin Watts, 1990.

Scopes, John Thomas, and Presley, James. *Center of the Storm.* New York: Holt, Rinehart and Winston, 1967.

Smith, Sherwin D. "The Great Monkey Trial." *New York Times Magazine,* July 4, 1965.

Stone, Irving. *Clarence Darrow for the Defense.* New York: Doubleday, 1941.

Tierney, Kevin. *Darrow: A Biography.* New York: Thomas Y. Crowell, 1979.

Index